# GOLD AND SILVER SCRAP DEALERS HANDBOOK

## V Alexander Cullen

### How to Cash In on the Precious Metals Bonanza.

**From the Author of Pawnbrokers Handbook**

~1~

*Gold and Silver Scrap Dealers Handbook:*
*How to Cash In on the Precious Metals*
*Bonanza*
*By V. Alexander Cullen*
*Copyright © 2011 by V. Alexander Cullen*

*This book is dedicated to the memory of my*
*Dad the "Colonel".*

# Contents......................

# Chapter 1

...........................................

## Gold and Silver

GOLD! Say the word and your mind instantly pictures the warm lustrous yellow metal. Few people can pick up a pure gold coin or ingot and not have a desire to own it. Over the centuries men have gone to every part of our planet searching for the yellow metal. They have suffered every hardship to dig it out of the earth. Whole continents have been conquered and millions killed to acquire vast hordes of gold. Kingdoms, nations and entire civilizations have arisen in the quest for more gold. Gold is power. It is a rare and beautiful metal but it is man's desire to possess it that gives it that power. Gold will buy almost anything. The number one rule about Gold is "Those who have the gold make the Rules". Naturally, everyone wants to own more gold so they can "make the Rules".

It is gold's rarity and man's hunger for more gold that causes a demand, creates value and makes it hard to get. As long as the world has "faith" in the American dollar you can buy all the gold and silver you want from dealers or mints but they will charge you retail price which is spot price plus a percentage. Spot price is determined on a daily basis on the worlds markets. We constantly see and hear all those ads on the television and radio trying to sell us gold. To be able to buy all those commercials, they must be making big bucks. The trading pits of the World's Commodity Markets are full of people who buy and sell huge amounts of gold, silver and other precious metals. You can invest in precious metals futures, calls, puts, hedge funds, mutual funds, mining stocks, etc...You can invest millions in gold, silver and precious metals and never even touch the actual metals. I like being able to hold my gold and silver in my hands. There must be an easier and cheaper way to acquire gold without paying retail price.

Gold can be had by prospecting and mining. This requires a lot of backbreaking labor and a substantial investment in tools and time. You must also travel to remote areas where someone hasn't already mined all the gold and suffer discomfort and danger. If you do actually find gold, it may cost you less than retail. If you don't find it, you lose the money and the time you invested, not mention the hard work and suffering. There are those among us who will kill and steal to get gold but this immoral and illegal. It could also be dangerous because there are also those among us, including myself, who will shoot back to protect ourselves and our gold. Only the government can legally steal your gold. Franklin Roosevelt did it in 1933 during the depression. He took our gold so he could make the "Rules". The good news is that there is an excellent way, my favorite way, to acquire gold and silver for less than the current retail price. It is legal, moral and so politically correct that even Al Gore should approve of it. Buy scrap gold and silver and then recycle it!

People all over the planet are being trained to recycle their paper, plastic, glass, aluminum and metal cans, why not gold and silver? They can bring it to me and I will pay them well to recycle their old gold and silver. Over the years, I have bought hundreds of ounces of scrap gold and silver and people are glad to be paid a fair price for items they no longer want or need. They get rid of their unwanted items to be recycled and I am able to buy gold and silver at less than retail prices. I am usually able to buy as low as half of current spot price. People want to be good stewards and recycle. They also like to be paid cash for stuff they no longer want. It's a good deal for them and a good deal for me. Nearly every adult in this nation has old gold and silver to recycle. They bring me broken, ugly, old fashioned gold and silver items. Items like old wedding bands, old class rings, broken chains, pendants, mismatched or single earrings, old charms, rings with missing stones and pins. I've seen Uncle John's Masonic ring, Aunt Emma's club pin, and Grandma's wedding band even dead relatives gold teeth. These items are 10K, 14K, 18K and Sterling. I've also seen 8K gold from England and 22K jewelry from Asia and the Middle East. I've also bought gold and silver coins. Folks have millions of ounces of gold rolling around in their drawers and jewelry boxes just waiting to be recycled. If every person in the United States could recycle just a quarter ounce of 14k gold, with 300 million people, that would be 43,875,000 ounces of pure gold. (300,000,000 x ¼ ounces x 58.5% (14K) = 43,875,000 pure gold) With spot prices at around $1380 per ounce, this would be worth $60.5 Billion. Yes that is Billion with a "B". That's a nice piece of change. If you could buy all that as scrap then there is a potential to make a $30 billion profit. Look out Bill Gates and Warren Buffet. Of course, in reality it may be difficult to get 300 million people to sell you their scrap. It might also be hard to come up with the $30 billion necessary to pay all your customers but an old allegory comes to mind. How do you eat an elephant? You just take one bite at a time. Most of us would settle for just one big bite of a $60 billion dollar elephant. I have been a Pawnbroker for almost twenty-five years and over the years, I've done my best to eat my share of that elephant.

## Gold and Silver History

Long before recorded history, there was gold. On the third day of Creation, when God made the dry land appear, the yellow metal that we call gold was in that dry land. All through the Bible are references to Gold and Silver. The King James Bible mentions gold 361 times. In Genesis 13:2 it says that Father Abraham "was rich in cattle, in silver, and in gold". The Bible mentions a golden calf, a golden statue in Babylon, Solomon's

~ 11 ~

gold and a gold covered Ark. Silver is referenced 282 times. The lords of the Philistines each gave Delilah eleven hundred pieces of silver to betray Samson, Judas betrayed Christ for just thirty. Archaeology confirms what the Bible says. The use of gold first started in the ancient Middle-East where civilization began. The world's oldest gold jewelry was found in the tombs of Egypt and Mesopotamia. The Persians gathered vast hordes of gold as did the Romans. Gold, slaves and tribute from conquered territories built many great civilization, massive cities and armies. The Spanish explored the New World of the Americas and conquered the great Pre-Columbian civilizations that lived there so they could haul away great shiploads of gold and silver. There were many "Gold Rushes" in the early days of the United States. The most famous was when gold was found at Sutter's Mill in 1848. Gold strikes also happened in Australia in 1851, South Africa in 1884 and the famous Yukon strike of Canada in 1897.

The use of Gold and Silver as money also goes back to ancient times. Mesopotamian merchants were accepting silver as money as early as 700 BC. The Egyptians were the first to use gold as money. The United States Congress based our currency on the silver dollar and its fixed relationship to gold. Our Constitution specifically says that "No State shall...make anything but gold and silver Coin a Tender in Payment of

~ 13 ~

Debts". Prior to the end of the nineteenth century, the currencies of most nations were based on the Gold Standard. In 1933 Franklin Roosevelt and congress outlawed the private ownership of gold except for jewelry. The Breton Woods System in 1946 created a system that allowed governments to sell their gold to the U.S. treasury at a fixed rate of $35 per ounce. This allowed world currencies to be linked to the value of gold. In 1971, Richard Nixon ended the Bretton Woods Agreement, allowed the private ownership of Gold and ended the fixed price trading of gold. The use of silver to mint U.S. Coins ceased with the Coinage Act of 1965. Just a few years ago the Swiss were the last nation to drop the Gold Standard. So what are the World's Currencies based upon in current times? It is based on nothing, except your good faith. You accept paper or electronic money for your labor, goods and services and have faith that everyone else in the world will accept the same money for the things that you need. As long as everyone has "faith" then things just keep bumping along. Do you have that kind of faith? Most people still do and while they still do, those of us who deal in scrap precious metals are able to exchange our paper currency for the proven money of the past, Gold and Silver.

# Chapter 2

........................................................

## Buying Gold and Silver Scrap

You don't have to be a Pawnbroker to buy scrap gold and silver. Anyone, with a little knowledge and a few tools, can make good money buying scrap gold and silver. Any one already in business can supplement that business buying scrap gold and silver. You can buy scrap gold and silver as a "side business" if you are employed by someone else. It is a great way to supplement a retirement income. Anyone can buy precious metals scrap but some states do require licensing. The latest fad is to have "Gold Buying Parties". People invite friends, relatives, coworkers and neighbors to clean out their junk drawers and jewelry boxes. They will come to the sponsor's home and sell their unwanted items for cash. You can have business cards made that explain what kind of items you are looking for and pass them out to any likely prospect. The gold and silver you buy as scrap can be sold to a refiner for cash or you can take payment in freshly minted gold and silver bullion coins for your own collection. There is another bonus. Many of the items you buy for scrap can be cleaned and repaired to be sold at retail. I have bought many items that required very little work to make them look like new and then sold them as jewelry. I am able to fix and polish jewelry myself but if you develop a relationship with a local jeweler you can have items that have potential for resale, polished and cleaned. He may even want to buy them from you to supplement his shop inventory. I have sold lots of scrap at current spot to jewelers who make their own jewelry. They especially like old wedding bands which are perfect to cut up to size other rings or to melt for castings. Many of the mounted stones in the items I buy for scrap are also saleable. Large diamonds have been regularly offered to me. Unlike gold and silver which can easily be evaluated for weight and content, diamonds are harder to judge. The diamond market is fickle and the scrap value of stones smaller than ½ carat crashed a few years ago. Even stones larger than ½ carat are worth less than they were 10 years ago. Be careful when investing in diamonds.

Jewelers are still buying small diamonds and other stones for repairs but when they can buy new ones cheaply, they want to pay even less used ones. I recommend buying jewelry with stones mounted mainly for the gold or silver content and if the piece looks like it could be resold as jewelry then pay a small premium for the value of the stone(s) and the value of the labor to mount it. I have seen many large semi-precious colored stones mounted in rings, pendants and pins that are as heavy as or heavier than the mounting they are in. In most cases, I will discount what I will pay for the scrap value of the item, if there is such a stone in it, to compensate for the weight of the stone.

On very rare occasions, a platinum

item will show up. Most of the platinum pieces I've seen are marked as 90% platinum. Platinum jewelry is usually the finest quality money can buy. If you can buy it for scrap prices try to buy it at the same ratio as gold or silver, about half of spot. Any platinum jewelry that is salvageable as jewelry will bring a premium price for resale. Most of the platinum jewelry I have come across is antique and estate pieces. When I wrote "Pawnbroker's Handbook" many years ago, silver stayed in the $4 to $6 per ounce range. Today it is hovering around $30 per ounce. At those prices, silver jewelry is more attractive to buy for scrap. It takes a lot of silver jewelry to be worth much though. Silver jewelry is usually marked "Sterling" or "925" and is 92.5% pure silver. If spot silver is $30 per ounce, there is $27.75 pure silver per ounce of "Sterling". If you divide that by 20 pennyweights per Troy ounce, then it's $1.39 per pennyweight pure silver value. I would offer about 70 cents per pennyweight. Large chains, heavy rings or a pile of smaller pieces can be worth dealing with. Coins, flatware and hollowware are even better. The following is an excerpt from "Pawnbrokers Handbook".

## COINS

*Coins can be a very profitable part of the pawn broking business. In my pawnshop, an entire showcase is devoted to a display of coins. I have everything from mint sets to culls for sale. A cull is a coin that is good only for* *its silver value. These coins are usually severely worn, but you will still be able to recognize them as U.S. coins. They may even have dates that are readable. These coins are traded in commodity markets by the bag and the half bag. A bag contains $1,000 face value worth of U.S. mint pre-1965 silver coins. They can be mixed denominations or of one denomination. Although most of the coins I see are culls, I do get some nice collector's pieces, mint sets, slabs, and complete collections.*

*It takes years of study and practice to become a certified numismatist who can professionally grade coins, and I cannot tell you everything about coins in this chapter. I can give you a few basics, but if you are not knowledgeable about* this subject, it would be in your best interest to learn more.

There are two ways to value coins. One is by their silver value, and the other is by their collector value. Try to make loans or buy coins based on their silver content only. If the coins you are dealing with are of better grades, then you must figure out the collector value, which means you must grade them to the best of your ability. One of the books I use is the Handbook of United States Coins by R.S. Yeoman, which lists dealer's buying prices. This and every good coin book has a section on how to grade coins. I find myself reading this section every time I look up a coin to refresh my memory. Most of the values are based not only on the amount of wear to the high points of the coin, but also on its date, where it was minted, and the number of coins minted in that batch. I see very few coins that are uncirculated, and most are valued at the lower to middle end of the scale. I will show customers the value of their coins listed in this book and offer them half of that for a loan and 10 percent more to buy them.

There is also a chart in the back of Yeoman's book that shows the bullion value for each type of coin. Using this chart, you can figure out the silver value for any U.S. coin. For example, if the spot price of silver is $4 per ounce, a pre-1965 silver half-dollar, which has about 1/3 ounce of silver in it, would be worth $1.45. I would offer $1 per coin

**Gold and Silver Scrap Dealers Handbook**

on a loan and $1.10 per coin to buy them. Most coin dealers will buy these coins for 15percent less than their silver value and sell them for 15 percent more than their silver value. I like to get them for a little less than 15 percent and sell them for a little more than 15 percent.

Notice that I haven't said much about non-silver coins, like pennies and nickels. The reason is that there is only a collector's market for these coins. Most Lincoln-head pennies and Jefferson nickels, except for a few rare series, are worth little more than 1 cent and 5 cents, respectively. Most coin dealers will sell Lincoln-head wheat pennies by the roll for slightly more than face value, and most Jefferson nickels end up in my cash register change drawer.

Appendix E lists coin buyers, but be prepared for your coins to be graded lower than you expect and get priced accordingly. When I sell coins, I always try to retail them in my showcase. I use a retail price book like the Official Blackbook Price Guide, which is available at your local bookstore, or the Littleton Coin Company's catalog.

## SILVERWARE

Silver flatware and hollowware are always in demand. They must, of course, be solid silver, because silver-plated items aren't worth much. I always value silverware by the actual silver content in the piece. I will weigh it on my scale and estimate how much

~ 26 ~

pure silver is in it. If I'm weighing a set of flatware, I will take each piece from a setting and weigh it, then multiply their weights by the number of settings there are. Large pieces of hollowware are sometimes too big to fit on my scale, so I must guess at the weight. Once I figure out the weight in troy ounces, I multiply this by the current spot price per ounce for pure silver. I also take into account that silverware is only 92.5 percent pure silver, which means I must adjust the spot price of silver by 92.5 percent. For example, if the spot price for silver is $4 per ounce, silverware is worth $3.70 per ounce. I would purchase it for $3 per ounce (about 80 percent of spot price) and loan $2.50 per ounce (about 70 percent of spot price).

*Atlantic Silver Incorporated (see Appendix E) offers a free pattern identification booklet. Rare patterns can sell for a premium, and even common patterns will sell for at least twice their silver value. Engraved initials will devalue silverware unless it belonged to a famous individual. The booklet also has pictures of trademarks and proof marks that can help you determine if a piece is solid silver. The main marks to look for that indicate if a piece is solid silver and not silver plate is the word "sterling" or the numbers 925 (92.5 percent).*

The information above is still applicable except that the value of silver has risen significantly by seven and half times. The cull silver half which had $1.45 worth of silver back then now has about $10.88 worth of silver with spot prices at $30 per ounce silver. I believe that silver has a tremendous upside potential. I can still remember my father buying silver like mad in his pawn shop when silver was $50 per ounce in the late seventies and early eighties. People were cashing in everything they could find with silver in it including grandma's silverware and grandpa's moustache cup. Gold was around $800 per ounce and Dad was shipping to the refiner at least once per week.

The following is Chapter 5 from the "Pawnbrokers Handbook". It was, of course, written as a "how to" book to open a Pawn Shop but it is also applicable to the Gold and Silver scrap dealer. As such, the majority of the items you will be buying and selling will be gold and silver jewelry. Selling every item you can as retail jewelry will maximize the profit potential of every dollar you invest. The prices were not changed because the price of gold can change in either direction. You will need to do the math

## Jewelry

*Gold. The word conjures up visions of prospectors digging large nuggets of yellow metal out of sluice pans or of a pirate's treasure glistening on a coral reef below azure waters. The discovery of gold in your pawnshop won't be quite as romantic, but you will not have to risk your life or even get dirty to profit from it. People will bring you all types of gold objects, and most of them will have some type of precious or semiprecious jewel in them. For your benefit, you should consider diamonds to be precious stones; rubies, sapphires and emeralds to be semiprecious; and everything else to be not worth much.*

*Learn all you can about diamonds, gems, and gold. It is helpful to go to other pawnshops and jewelry stores to see what they charge for their jewelry. Go to large jewelers and ask to look at their diamonds. It is also good to keep on hand several discount department store catalogs that have color pictures of their jewelry. I find that I can buy most jewelry for about 10 cents on the dollar of what it sold for new. I can*

~ 31 ~

*usually sell it for 50 percent or less than what the jewelry stores ask. Even the discount chains like Wal-Mart and Kmart can't compete with that. Below are the basic tools you will need to weigh, measure, and otherwise work with gold jewelry, diamonds, and other gems.*

*scales*

*electronic gold tester*

*electronic diamond tester*

*10X loupe*

*accurate diamond gauge*

*Moe diamond gauge and calculator*

*ultrasonic jewelry cleaner*

*buffing machine and accessories*

*ring clamp*

*needle-nose pliers*

*jeweler's saw and blades*


*At the top of the list are scales. You will need scales that meet legal-for-*

*trade specifications for your state. They should weigh grams, troy ounces, and pennyweight. They need not be the most expensive, but they should be sturdy and durable. You will likely be using them every day. When shopping for this equipment, I usually buy models that fall in the middle of the price range. I provide several sources for jeweler's supplies in Appendix C.*

Equipment for weighing gold and evaluating diamonds.

*I still have the Ohaus triple beam scales that I started out with more than nine years ago. They still work perfectly but are slow and tedious to use. I've been spoiled since I acquired my digital scales. It's nice to have an instant reading of weight without changing little weights and sliding little scales and reading hash marks to get an exact measurement. That's why I suggested that you buy a modern scale with a digital readout.*

*As far as which weight system to use, I recommend that you use troy. I was trained in the troy system, and I don't care much for gram measurements. Gold is always traded in the world markets in troy ounces. Sometimes you may have to convert to gram weight for your customers, but digital scales can do this, which is another good reason to own one. Some pawnbrokers buy and sell by gram weight, and customers may be price shopping. Also, many of the discount jewelers sell their gold by the gram. Here are some basics:*

*One troy pound = 12 troy ounces*
*One troy ounce = 20 pennyweight (dwt)*
*One pennyweight = 24 grains*
*15.43 grains = one gram (gm)*
*One gram = 1.6 pennyweight (approx.)*
*31.1 grams = one troy ounce*

*GOLD*

*If you want to be a successful pawnbroker, you will need to follow the* price of gold carefully. The London market sets the daily price per troy ounce for gold in the world markets. This is referred to as the London "fix" and it is done twice a day. This price is for the spot market, which means this is the price you will pay if you take possession of the gold that day. This daily price quote is reported on radio and television financial programs and is published in the newspaper under metal commodities. These quotes will determine what you should pay and, to some extent, what you can sell your scrap gold and retail jewelry for. Though gold is traded in the market in troy ounces, the main unit of measurement you need to be concerned about is the pennyweight. Almost all the buying and selling of gold in your *pawnshop will be done by pennyweight.*

*How Much to Pay for Gold*

*How much you pay for gold in your pawnshop should be determined more by what you can scrap it for and less by what you think you may be able to retail it for as jewelry. It's true I will pay more for a nice resalable piece of jewelry than a piece that is good only for scrap, but I always pay less than gold value at the current market rate. To figure out the gold value for a specific piece of jewelry, you must begin by looking at the current market price. For example, if the current market price is $368 per troy ounce, you must divide by 20 to get the price per pennyweight*

~ 37 ~

(dwt), which is $18.40. You should consider the profit margin of the refiner to which you will sell it. (Some refiners are listed in Appendix C.) Most refiners will pay at least 95 percent of spot price for a 5 percent profit margin. (The amount will vary according to the amount you scrap, and there are sometimes other fees involved.) So $18.40 per pennyweight multiplied by 95 percent is $17.48. This is what you can realistically expect to sell gold for in the spot market on this particular day. You must also figure that on the day you actually sell your gold, the price may have changed. What will the price be tomorrow? If I were able to predict the answer to that question, I could be as rich as Ross Perot.

**Gold and Silver Scrap Dealers Handbook**

*The price of gold fluctuates due to the influence of many different forces. Sometimes emotion or panic in world markets, political upheavals, and wars can affect prices. A strike in a gold-producing state like South Africa or a shooting war in an oil producing state like Kuwait will cause gold prices to go up. A big sell-off of gold by Russia or a large bank will cause gold prices to go down. Gold has always been used as a hedge against inflation, and this can also have a big effect on prices. You have no control over these things, so you must watch trends in the market and situations in the world to determine what percentage of spot market price you are willing to pay.*

*When you are in the gold business, it*

pays to watch the news. You must also consider that, at least in most cases, the gold you get from your customers is not pure gold; it is mixed with alloys. You will occasionally see gold bullion or gold coins, but mostly you get karat gold in the form of jewelry. European-made jewelry will be marked with the percentage of pure gold contained in the piece instead of a karat mark (k) like American jewelry. Here is a listing of karat marks and corresponding European marks and percentages of pure gold:

| U.S.A. | European | Percentage |
|---|---|---|
| 24k | 999 | 99.9 |
| 18k | 750 | 75 |
| 14k | 585 | 58.5 |
| l0k | 417 | 41.7 |
| 8k | 333 | 33.3 |

~ 40 ~

*Since the Persian Gulf War, I have seen a lot of 22k gold jewelry that was brought back by servicemen from Saudi Arabia. These pieces are sometimes marked as 90 percent, or 900. There is also dental gold (yes, people really do take the gold out of dead people's teeth), which is usually 16k or 65 percent gold.*

*Once you figure out what karat gold you are working with, you have to decide how much per pennyweight you want to pay for it. For example, a customer brings you a 10k yellow gold class ring with a red stone in it, and it weighs in at 10 dwt. The red stones in 99percent of all class rings are synthetic rubies and are worth practically nothing* for scrap. You must estimate the weight of the stone and deduct that amount from the total weight of the ring. If the stone weighs 1.5 dwt, then the gold in the ring weighs 8.5 dwt. Next, you will need to figure the price per dwt for 10k gold, which is 41.7 percent pure gold. $17.48 per dwt (the previously determined gold value for that day) times 41.7 percent equals $7.29 per dwt. This is the price per pennyweight you will receive from the refiner on the day he receives it from you if the spot price is $368 per ounce. I will normally pay $3.50 to $4.50 per pennyweight for a ring like this. This works out to $30 for a loan, or $35 to $40 to buy it. This leaves me room to still make a profit even if gold goes down in value.

*I always try to buy and pawn jewelry at prices that enable me to make a profit at scrap. If I am able to sell a piece at retail, then it's a big bonus. Retail jewelry can bring double or triple its scrap value. If you do decide to send gold to a refiner for scrap, you should wait until you have at least 100 dwt. My refiner pays up to 95 percent of spot price on shipments over 100 dwt.*

*At the prices discussed earlier, I would receive about $62 ($7.29 x 8.5 = $61.97) for the class ring. I could make as much as a $32 profit on this ring if he doesn't redeem it, or if he leaves it in pawn and pays interest, I could make $6.80 per month. In just five months, I can make even more than if I had* scrapped it. Here are some formulas to use when trading in gold:

Spot price of gold ÷ 20 dwt = spot price per dwt.

Spot price per dwt x karat percentage = karat price per dwt.

Karat price per dwt x 95 percent = price per dwt from refiner.

I don't usually go through all these calculations. Instead, I rely on the following table unless I have a difficult customer who has had offers from other dealers and I must offer a better price.

10k $3 to $3.50 per dwt
14k $5 to $5.50 per dwt
18k $6.50 to $7 per dwt
22k $8 to $8.50 per dwt
24k $9 to $10 per dwt

*I have been pawning and buying gold for more than nine years, and spot prices have varied from just under $300 per ounce to just over $400 per ounce. I have always paid about the same prices that are listed above, and I have always made a profit.*

## Testing for Fakes

*It may look like gold, feel like gold, and even be marked with a karat mark, but it still may turn out not to be gold. Even after years of experience, I have been fooled.*

*With the new electronic gold testers*

~ 45 ~

that are now on the market, testing gold is fast, easy, and accurate. The tester I have works by placing the piece to be tested on a tray and attaching an alligator clip, which is wired to the positive lead, to the piece. The negative lead is wired through a tube that contains a special gel. Twisting the back of this tube dispenses a drop of this gel, and the authenticity and karat value of the piece is tested by touching the drop of gel away from the point where the piece contacts the alligator clamp. You then press the test button to get a numerical reading, which is compared to a scale that gives you a karat value. This is a vast improvement over the old method of acid testing.

Gold Tester.

*To acid test a piece of gold, you must have a file and some nitric acid. You must file into the piece to get through any layers of gold plating and then apply the acid to the bare metal. Gold will keep the acid clear, silver will turn it yellow, and other metals will turn it green. To determine the karat value, the piece must be rubbed on a*

~ 47 ~

touchstone, acid applied, and the colors interpreted. These methods are time consuming and inaccurate. Even if you can file an area that won't be noticed, you will still leave an ugly mark on the jewelry. Some customers won't allow you to do this to their jewelry, which leaves you with the choice to either not take it or not test it.

For years, I got by without using an electronic tester, but if I had tested a few of the fakes I took, the tester would have easily paid for itself. Most of the time, I can tell that a piece is real, but if there is any question in my mind at all, I run it on my tester. I highly recommend that you buy an electronic gold tester and use it often until you gain enough experience to do without it.

It is also a good idea to weigh the jewelry and reach an agreement with the customer for a price before you do your testing. After you've had enough experience, you will be able to tell the good from the bad about 99 percent of the time. Most gold-plated jewelry will be marked as such. Some of these markings are:

1/10 12k (14k, 18k, 24k) G.F.
1/20 12k (14k, 18k, 24k) G.F.
G.F.
Gold Filled
R.G.P.
Rolled Gold Plated
Heavy Gold Electroplate
10k, 14k, 18k, or 24k H.G.E.

When you see a piece marked 14kp or 18kp, it doesn't mean that it is plated, but that it is "plumb" gold. Plumb means that the gold content is exactly the karat marked. In 1976, Congress amended the National Gold and Silver Act, and by 1981, all American gold manufacturers had to adhere to the stricter standards for gold content in their jewelry. Previously, for example, jewelry manufacturers could mark their jewelry as 14k when it was actually only 13k. Since 1981, all American jewelry manufacturers have marked their jewelry with the plumb designation.

Sometimes you will encounter silver jewelry that is gold plated. This is also called gold overlay. This type of jewelry isn't usually marked as plated but is marked with the designation 925. This means the piece is 92.5 percent silver.

Look for plated jewelry to show peeling and wear if it's been worn often. These things will show even better if you look at it closely with your loupe.

In my experience, gold chains are the items most often faked. Most gold chains are soldered on their ends, or, at the very least, the ring that attaches the clasp to the chain is soldered. While this isn't always proof positive that you have the genuine article, it is a good indicator. I have taken fake chains that look real even to the soldered ends. The last ones I took seemed to tarnish after I kept them the required 30 days.

When I took them in, I failed to test them with my acid (I didn't have an electronic tester at the time). They were marked 14k, and they had nice lobster-claw clasps on them, but they were not gold. They were evidently gold-plated brass that was made specifically to rip off people like me who buy gold. This $275 lesson was enough to convince me to buy an electronic gold tester. From then on, any piece of jewelry, especially chains, that weighs more than 5 dwt or that wasn't previously pawned by a regular customer gets checked on my electronic gold tester.

Other frequently faked items are gold watches. There are a few problems that can be encountered. Gold watches are hard to authenticate even with a gold tester. The tester may damage the delicate moving parts or the crystal of the watch. Only the case of the watch is actually gold and can't be weighed accurately unless you take the moving parts out, which is impractical.

If the customer gives you permission to file a small notch where the band is attached underneath the watch, you can put a tiny amount of acid in the notch to check for a reaction. You must take the band off to do this, and you must be careful not to damage the watch. If the band is soldered to the watch and is marked as gold, you can usually put the band in your electronic tester and get an accurate reading. Again, get permission from the customer, and let him or her know that you can't be responsible for damage, though you will do your best not to do any.

*If a customer won't let you test his watch in these ways, you may want to pass on it unless you can get it cheap. It is always best to stay low in your pricing on gold watches so you can't get burned by a fake. Any watch that has a stainless steel back, except a Rolex, is not gold. If you can test the diamonds and they are good, then this is usually a sign that the watch is gold, if it is marked as such. You will see many more ladies' watches than men's watches, and luckily they aren't faked as often. The best advice I can give on watches is to be careful. There are huge profits to be made on watches, but if you get a fake, there are also huge losses to be suffered.*

*If you are not well acquainted with*

*jewelry, it is in your best interest to check most everything that comes into your shop until you are confident that you can spot fakes. Even then, you will want to check anything that looks suspicious in any way. It only takes a loss on one fake to cancel out the profit on several good deals.*

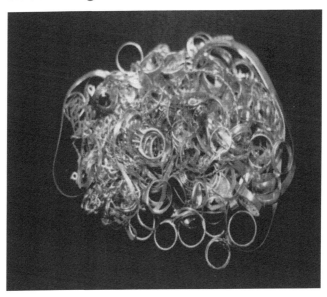

Gold! These pieces are headed for the refinery.

## Scrapping Gold for Cash

Selling your gold to a refiner is a good, dependable source of quick cash when you need it. Though I try to sell my scrap gold when the market price is high, I am not always able to hold out for the best price. Most of the time, I end up selling right before my quarterly estimated income tax is due, but sometimes I hold out to hit a peak in market prices. I recently sent off a batch of scrap to my refiner and got a check back for more than $6,000. I hit a market price of around $380 per ounce. I had been holding out for a higher price, but when it peaked at just over $400 per ounce then fell back down, I jumped in and sold. If I had sold when the market was $20 per ounce higher, I *could have made an extra $200. All the same, I made at least a $2,700 profit on this sale.*

*You should try to save every piece of jewelry you can to fill your jewelry showcases with merchandise for retail. I scrap only what I can't use in this capacity, which includes broken and kinked chains, class rings, wedding bands, rings that are worn or broken, and any other jewelry that isn't suitable for sale. I will also, on occasion, take a diamond out of its mounting to scrap (this is covered later) and use the mounting for gold scrap. Some pawnbrokers try to sell wedding bands for retail, but I find them hard to sell and mostly use them for scrap.*

## DIAMONDS

Diamonds conjure up visions of wealth and beauty. They inspire awe and mystery in people. Most people consider them to be the most valuable objects in the world, but diamonds are nothing but rocks, mere pieces of stone. When cut and polished correctly, they are things of beauty, but there is nothing mysterious or magical about them. The fact that they are valuable and expensive is a testament to the public relations campaign put on by the De Beers diamond cartel. I won't get into the saga of the De Beers family or a history of the diamond industry, but it is sufficient to say they are responsible for making the diamond what it is today.

*The De Beers control 90 percent of the entire world's diamonds, either in their own vaults or in the countries where the world's diamonds are produced. By controlling supply and, through continuous commercial campaigns, demand, this diamond cartel has kept the price of diamonds artificially high. Everyone knows diamonds are forever, diamonds are a girl's best friend, and that if a man loves a woman he must give her a diamond. The De Beers have convinced us that diamonds are extremely rare, when in reality they are only rare because the diamond cartel strictly controls supply. If the diamond cartel ever ceases to exist, the price of diamonds would probably fall close to*

~ 59 ~

*the price of rubies, sapphires, and emeralds.*

*Watch the news and trade magazines for anything about Russian diamonds. I have heard rumors about them dumping diamonds on the world market. The Russians have more diamonds stockpiled than any other country or organization (including De Beers), and they are in terrible financial shape. If they begin dumping, the price of diamonds could plummet. This could have a bad effect on your business, cause people to lose confidence in diamonds, and wreck the whole diamond industry.*

*In the meantime, you can make large amounts of money buying and selling* diamonds. Since the De Beers cartel controls the supply of diamonds, they also control the price. There is no spot market or London fix for diamonds like there is for gold. You can't check the TV or the local newspaper for a daily quote on the price of diamonds.

The price of diamonds is affected by the famous four "Cs." These are carat, color, clarity, and cut. Of course, the price of a raw uncut diamond is only affected by the last three Cs, but you will likely never see a raw diamond, so I will explain the basics about finished diamonds. The basics should be enough to get you started, but I recommend that you read the books listed in Appendix C for more detailed information, because it would take volumes to teach everything about this subject.

Let me first deal with what a carat is. Notice that it is spelled with a "c" and not a "k." Diamonds are weighed in carats, and the content of gold in a piece of jewelry is measured in karats. It is not necessary to buy a scale to weigh diamonds, because most times you will be dealing with mounted stones, and you can only estimate the weight if the stone is attached to a ring. It would be convenient to have a carat scale to weigh loose stones, but I have always gotten by without one. A carat is broken down into points so that 1 ct equals 100 pts. The corresponding fractional carats are also broken down into points. These are:

*7/8 ct = 85 to 90 pts*

*3/4 ct = 75 pts*

*3/5 ct = 60 pts*

*1/2 ct = 50 pts*

*3/8 ct = 40 pts*

*1/3 ct = 33 pts*

*1/4 ct = 25 pts*

*1/5 ct = 20 pts*

*1/8 ct = 12 pts*

*1/10 ct = 10 pts*

*Color*

*The next thing to consider is color. Diamonds come in several colors besides white. I have seen diamonds as blue as sapphires, as brown as rusty water, as green as emeralds, and as yellow as sunflowers. These are usually called* fancy-color diamonds, and they can be worth more than their counterpart, which is white. Most of the stones I see that have color are not fancy colored but just off color. This is not a good thing. I always pay less for off color diamonds. The closer a diamond is to being colorless the better. I'm sure you've heard of diamonds being blue/white. This doesn't mean the diamond has a blue tint but that it is nearly colorless. Color can have a big effect on the value of a diamond, maybe even more than the other Cs. The Gemological Institute of America (GIA), an appraiser's association, rates the color of diamonds on a scale from D through Z+.

| D E F | G H I J | K L M N O P Q | R S T U V | W X Y Z Z+ |
|-------|---------|---------------|-----------|------------|
| color-less | near colorless | faint yellow | very light yellow | light yellow |

## Clarity

The third factor to consider when buying diamonds is clarity. When diamonds were formed millions of years ago, most of them trapped small particles of carbon inside. These flaws look like tiny pieces of coal, air spaces, fractures, or small feathers.

If no flaws can be seen with a 10X loupe, then the diamond is said to be flawless. There is really no such thing as a flawless diamond, because if you have a strong enough microscope, flaws can be seen in every diamond. The following is the GIA scale for clarity and the corresponding descriptions:

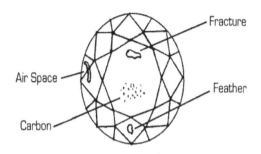

Air Space

Carbon

Fracture

Feather

## Clarity Grade                    Description

F
(Flawless)

No visible inclusions at 10X. Okay on tiny natural (part of the original surface of the diamond that is not removed when the stone is polished), but nothing visible internally or externally.

IF
(Internally
Flawless)

Very minor surface blemish removable with recut or polishing. Value usually at weight of recut gem.

VVS1
(Very Very
Slightly Included)

No table involvement. Very tiny pit, scratch, embedded crystal (must be under crown facets).

VVS 2 (Very Very Slightly Included)

One tiny inclusion: pit, spot, cleave, feather, abrasion, small extra facet.

VS1 (Very Slightly Included)

Combination totaling two tiny spots table: crystal, bearding (tiny fractures on the girdle), fracture, cleavage, bigger natural, scratch group.

VS2 (Very-Slightly Included)

Combination totaling three table inclusions, if not in the center: cluster, bigger crystal, feather, bearding more prominent. Large extra facets.

SI1 (Slightly-Included)

Combination totaling four of the following: series of nicks, Scratch group, inclusion cluster, small spot group in center of table.

SI2 (Slightly-

Combination totaling five of the: following inclusions in table center,

| Included) | major flaws cloudy area, inclusion cluster, large embedded crystals, carbon spots, cleavage visible. |
|---|---|
| I1 (Included) | Combination totaling six of the following: dead spots in stone (area that block reflected light), cleavages, feathers, embedded crystals, carbon spots, cloudy sections |
| I2 to I3 (Included) | Lowest GIA clarity grades. Any combination of inclusions totaling seven or more. |

## Cut

The final C is cut. The way a diamond is cut can mean the difference between a brilliant sparkle of reflected light and a dull fish-eye appearance. The cut of a diamond probably has the least effect

on its price but is still an important
factor. Modern faceting machines are
now used to cut diamonds, but fallible
men run them. There are precise
specifications for every style of
diamond cut, but these measurements
are often impossible for the diamond
cutter to achieve. The diamond cutter
tries to end up with the largest stone he
can get from a raw diamond, but he
must also try to cut off any flaws he
can. Sometimes the result is less than
perfect and can affect the value of the
stone.

Evaluating Diamonds

There is a standard procedure I use to
evaluate a diamond ring to be pawned
or sold. I check the karat marking and
weigh the piece to determine its gold

~ 69 ~

*value. If the mark is difficult to read, I use my 10X loupe.*

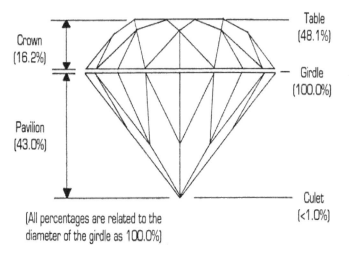

Crown
(16.2%)

Table
(48.1%)

Girdle
(100.0%)

Pavilion
(43.0%)

Culet
(<1.0%)

(All percentages are related to the
diameter of the girdle as 100.0%)

*With my loupe still at hand, I use it and my diamond gauge to estimate the approximate weight of the stone. By holding the gauge over the diamond, looking at it through my loupe, and moving the gauge until I find the hole that the diamond completely fills, I can make a fairly accurate guess on the*

~ 70 ~

*weight of the stone. The stone must completely fill the hole, leaving no space around the edge. The gauge gives readings in points. Occasionally, I get a ring that is marked inside with its weight in points. When I find this, it gives me a good idea of how accurately I'm estimating the weight of diamonds using my gauge. When a ring has more than one diamond, I estimate the weight of each one, and then add these together for a total weight. Sometimes it's hard to get the gauge right on top of small diamonds, so I get as close as possible or sometimes next to the stone and compare the stone to the holes and take a guess. I find that in most cases, diamonds in clusters have even sizes like 1/4 ct, 1/2 ct, 1 ct, etc.*

When I look at a stone with my loupe, I also check for flaws and damage. Always check very carefully for damage, especially around the girdle of the stone. The girdle is the part of a diamond that is easiest to damage. This area is very thin, and people chip their diamonds through abuse or neglect and never even realize they've done it. I have also seen chips in diamonds that occurred either before or during mounting and were hidden under a prong. A diamond that is chipped is worth considerably less than one of equal quality that is not chipped. A severely chipped diamond can be almost worthless.

Severely included diamonds are also something to watch out for. In the past *couple of years, I've seen more of what I call "promotional diamonds." These are really trashy stones of such poor quality that they look like cut and polished gravel. They are usually cut in countries where labor is extremely cheap, like India, Pakistan, or Thailand. I will take these pieces in pawn, but I base the amount given for them mainly on the gold weight. I rarely find diamonds that don't have some kind of flaw, and I can't ever recall getting any diamonds that meet the GIA criteria for a flawless rating. I usually figure that minor flaws in stones smaller than 20 pts have little effect on value. When the stone is larger than 20 pts, flaws start to make a big difference.*

*I also make a judgment about the cut*

~ 73 ~

and color of a diamond while estimating its weight and looking for flaws. These are difficult qualities to appraise unless you've been to GIA School. To check the color of a diamond, place a piece of white paper behind it, and look at it under good natural light.

## How Much to Pay for Diamonds

The value of a diamond increases geometrically according to its size, not arithmetically. For example, a 1-ct diamond could be worth four times as much as a 1/2-ct diamond of equal quality instead of twice as much, even though it is only twice as large. I use a pricing scale similar to the one shown below:

| Weight | Price |
|---|---|
| 1 pt to 20 pts | 25 cents to $1 per pt |

| | |
|---|---|
| 20 pts to 25 pts | 50 cents to $2 per pt |
| 25 pts to 50 pts | $1 to $4 per pt |
| 50 pts to 75 pts | $2 to $5 per pt |
| 75 pts to 100 pts | $3 to $7 per pt |
| 100 pts and larger | $4 to $10 per pt (more for a stone larger than 2 ct) |

These prices are, of course, for individual stones and not for the total weight of a cluster. For example, a customer comes into my store with a ladies' 25-pt solitaire engagement ring that weighs 1 pennyweight. The stone has a few specks of carbon but is cut well and appears to be near colorless. I offer the customer $40 for a loan and $50 to buy it. (Before handing over the *cash, check the stone on the diamond tester by touching the diamond with the probe on the tester while holding the ring.) If the ring became available for sale, I would put it in my showcase and ask $200 for it, or I could scrap it for $70 to $100. If the ring had a cluster of five stones that had the same total weight, I would offer $20 for a loan and $25 to buy it. It would retail in my showcase for $60 to $75 and scrap for $30 or $40.*

*When it comes to larger diamonds like 1/3 ct, ½ ct, 3/4 ct, 1 ct, and larger, your knowledge of diamonds becomes more important. I can buy a 1/3-ct stone for $60, a 1/2-ct stone for $150 to $200, a 3/4-ct stone for $250 to $350, and a 1-ct stone for $500 to $700.*

*The largest stone I ever bought was a 1 1/2-ct heart-shaped diamond. It was cut well and was really white, and I paid $1,500 for it. Of course, my wife liked it, so I gave it to her.*

## Scrapping Diamonds

Diamonds can be scrapped just like gold, though the selection of buyers is more limited. When scrapping diamonds, you must be extremely careful not to chip or otherwise damage them when removing them from their mountings. You will need a ring clamp, needle-nose pliers, and a jeweler's saw.

Rings with Tiffany-style four- or six-prong mountings are easy to remove. Tightly clamp the ring in the ring clamp

~ 77 ~

and, using the pliers, carefully pry the prongs away from the diamond. Gold is a soft metal and bends fairly easily, so you don't have to be Arnold Schwarzenegger to bend it. When the diamond becomes loose, dump it into a small Zip lock bag. Be careful not to drop it on the floor, because once on the ground, diamonds are very hard to find. I have dropped several small diamonds around my jewelry bench and never found them.

Diamonds mounted in other ways usually have to be cut out with a jeweler's saw. If you are going to scrap a ring, don't worry about tearing it up to get the diamond out. Just be concerned about damaging the diamond. The saw blade won't cut the diamond, *although the diamond will dull the blade in a hurry. Try to cut only the metal holding the diamond in the mount. I sometimes find it helpful to use an engraving tool with a flat point to finish cutting the stones loose. If you have a large stone you want to scrap but are afraid to cut it out of the mounting, most of the buyers I list in Appendix C will take it out for you and pay you for the scrap. The only disadvantage is that you won't get top dollar for your scrap gold. A short course in jewelry repair would teach this process.*

*One more thing—is sure to use your diamond tester before buying any diamonds. It is really embarrassing to send a diamond off for scrap only to be informed that it is a fake.*

~ 79 ~

*RUBIES, SAPPHIRES, AND EMERALDS*

*When buying or pawning gold jewelry with rubies, sapphires, or emeralds in them, I don't add much over the price of the gold in which they are mounted. The reason is that I have not found a buyer for these stones as scrap, and I value jewelry more for its scrap value than its artistic value. Don't get me wrong, these are rare and desirable gems, and they are salable as jewelry, but they must be acquired cheaply to be profitable. There are also a lot of fakes out there. A diamond can be tested on a diamond tester, and gold can be tested on a gold tester, but colored gems are hard to authenticate. You almost have to be a gemologist to distinguish the*

~ 80 ~

real from the fake colored gemstones.

## Evaluating Colored Gems

I use my diamond gauge to size colored gems, but the holes in it do not give an accurate estimate of their weight, because they are calibrated for diamonds. Colored gems are weighed in carats, but a carat of diamonds is different from a carat of colored gems. Like a diamond, the weight of a colored gem has an effect on its value, and its value tends to grow geometrically with its size. In my opinion, though, size doesn't make a difference until a gem weighs more than half a carat. I also think emeralds are worth about 10 percent more than both rubies and sapphires. Burma and Thailand dump

~ 81 ~

tons of rubies and sapphires on the world markets every year. Most of the world's emeralds come from South America and seem to be much rarer.

The four Cs that apply to diamonds are also important to the value of colored gemstones. Color is very important. After all, they are colored gems. The color of gems can be enhanced by heat and chemicals, and this is another good reason not to put too much money into them. As far as clarity goes, it is better to have a few flaws in a colored gem, because this can be an indication of its authenticity. Man-made gems can be made with flaws but generally are not. As far as cut goes, it has the least effect on the gem's value. Most all the colored gems I've seen lately are cut in Asia where the labor is cheap. These are, for the most part, pretty good stones, but I have seen some slop. Carat weight, of course, is also a factor.

## How Much to Pay for Colored Gems

Below is a chart that I use to figure what to pay for colored gems. When I refer to the size in points, I mean the points as indicated by my diamond gauge, which is not the actual weight of these stones.

| Stone Size | Price per Stone |
|---|---|
| 1 pt to 5 pts | 25 cents to 50 cents per stone |
| 5 pts to 10 pts | 50 cents to $1 per stone |
| 10 pts to 25 pts | $1 to $5 per stone |

| | |
|---|---|
| *25 pts to 50 pts* | *$5 to $20 per stone* |
| *50 pts and larger* | *$20 or more per stone* |

*To me, buying these colored gems is like shooting craps. You put your money down, roll the dice, and take your chances. But there is good money to be made if you get a good piece for a low price. If you can buy colored gems at the prices I suggest, it is hard to lose money. For example, I recently purchased an emerald ring that had a large, carat-sized, emerald-cut emerald with two triangular-shaped diamonds on each side, and it was mounted in an 18k gold ring. The diamonds tested as real and appeared to weigh about 25 pts together. I figured that I would give the customer about $25 for the diamonds.*

*The 18k gold mounting weighed more than 2 dwt for an additional $15 dollars. The emerald had a nice green color to it and a few small visible flaws. It appeared to be real—I'd seen many man-made emeralds and their color was usually darker—so I added another $35 for the emerald for a total of $75. After keeping the ring for the required number of days, I put it out for sale for $395. Eventually, I sold it to the girl who works for me for $250. She took the ring down the street to a local appraiser, who estimated the ring's value at more than $1,000. Needless to say, she was very happy.*

*There is good money to be made with these colored gems, but until you have gained experience, be careful.*

*Don't worry about a customer walking away because you made a low offer. Normally, you can buy these pieces for your price, and there will be someone else right behind the customer who walked away who is willing to sell to you.*

## OTHER STONES

*Stones like topaz, pearls, opals, and amethyst are valued mainly for the gold in their mountings or the diamonds around them. You will see the large quartz type stones like topaz and amethyst mounted in 10k and 14k rings. Some of these stones can be more than an inch wide and quite heavy. These pieces should be purchased mainly for their gold, and the approximate weight* of the stone should be deducted. Generally, if the stone is smaller than the largest ring in my diamond gauge, I will not deduct its weight. If it is between that size and the size of a dime, I will deduct 1 or 2 dwt. If the stone is larger than a dime, I will deduct 3 or 4 dwt. For instance, if the ring weighs 10 dwt, and the stone weighs 3 or 4 dwt, you should only pay for 5 or 6 dwt.

If the stones are smaller and look attractive, I will usually count them as part of the gold weight. Or, if the amount I come up with is a dollar or two short of an even number, I will usually add enough to make a round number. For instance, if I have a ring with an opal that weighs enough to give $18, I

~ 87 ~

will usually offer an even $20 if I think I can sell the ring as jewelry.

I always buy these rings at prices that allow a profit if they must be scrapped. If they look nice enough, I will try to sell them first because I can usually get about twice their scrap value this way. Any rings that have a scratched or damaged stone will almost always wind up in the scrap pile.

## WATCHES

There are few modern wristwatches that sell well in my pawnshop. Every drug store, grocery store, and discount store in the country sells wristwatches, and the market is flooded with this cheap junk. Men's and ladies' digital and cheap quartz analog watches are very hard to sell. People can buy new watches for as little as $10 that look good and will last for a year. When their cheap watch stops working, they just go and buy a new one. Because of this, I have stopped taking all but a few select models of watches. Rolex, Seiko, Citizen, and other high-quality models are all that are worth taking.

Rolex watches are always in great demand. I will purchase and make loans on all the good clean Rolexes I can get. I will loan 25 to 30 percent of their new retail price and purchase them for 5 percent more than that if the watch is like new and in the box. Rolexes retail for as much as $12,000 or more. Most of the ones I see are the average stainless-steel models, and I will offer $300 to $400 for a loan on these. If you don't know what Rolexes sell for, go to a local dealer and get a price list. Don't tell him you're a pawnbroker, but ask him what his best cash price would be for both a man's and a lady's mid-range model like a stainless steel Datejust. If he will discount them, and most dealers will, you can adjust the prices on the list by this percentage and have a good idea what a new Rolex costs.

Beware of fake Rolexes. There are a lot of them around. Most fake Rolexes have quartz movements and a hesitating second hand that stops at every second, which gives them away. There are fake Rolexes around with self-winding movements just like the real ones, and

~ 90 ~

*the only way to be sure it's a genuine Rolex is to remove the wristband and look for its serial number. Always get the customer's permission before you do this, and make sure you don't scratch or damage the watch. Push a straight pin into the holes on each side of the lugs to compress the spring-loaded pin that attaches the wristband to the watch. There should be numbers stamped in the case on each side where the band was. The number without any letters in it is usually the serial number. The wristband of a real Rolex will also have a number on the underside of the clasp mechanism. If the watch is gold or gold and stainless steel, the number will be marked on the case and the band as 14 or 18 without a "k."*

*Seiko and Citizen are also good brands, but, unlike Rolexes, they are sold by all the discount stores. Therefore, the catalogs for these stores are good places to reference prices for these watches. I am mainly interested in men's and ladies' sports watches that retail new for more than $150. The Seiko and Citizen diver's and pilot's watches are especially good. I will loan 15 to 25 percent of their new retail price and purchase them for 5 percent more than that if they are like new and in the box.*

*There are also collectible Swiss and American watches. They are rare, and if you get one that you think might be valuable, it is best to contact one of the watch buyers I list in Appendix C. They* will help you evaluate it and may even be interested in buying it from you. Good collectible pocket watches are scarce these days. Ten years ago, there were lots of good vintage pocket watches around, but I'm lucky to see one or two per year now. The value of pocket watches can be hard to determine. Most of them can be pawned or purchased for $25 to $100 and can be sold for double or triple that amount. The best way to test a pocket watch is to have the customer bring it in unwound and not running. When the watch is wound all the way up and starts running, it is a good sign that it works. The fact that it ran well enough to unwind the main spring is proof that it will keep time.

~ 93 ~

One thing to consider with pocket watches and wristwatches is if they run and keep time. Unless you are a watchmaker, there are few things you can do short of wearing or carrying the watch. Usually, if a customer comes in wearing a watch and it has the correct time and date on it, then it is probably good. If the time or date is incorrect, beware. Always avoid dirty, beat-up watches with scratched crystals, because people won't buy them. Watches can be very expensive to repair, especially vintage pocket watches. Try to get an estimate before you commit to having one fixed, because some cost more to fix than they are worth. Find a good watchmaker in your area who will fix your watches at dealer's rates.

## PREPARING YOUR JEWELRY FOR SALE

*After several months in business, you will begin to accumulate a lot of good jewelry to sell. As soon as you open your doors for business and have all the proper licenses to buy and pawn gold, try to get all the jewelry you can to start filling your showcases. Almost all the jewelry you get will need to be cleaned or polished or both. Some of it will need to be repaired. The jewelry supply companies listed in Appendix C carry many books and videos on jewelry repair in their catalogs. Jewelry repair is not absolutely necessary to know, but you should learn how to polish jewelry. Your jewelry will sell much better if it is clean and presented professionally.*

~ 95 ~

*Many jewelers' schools are also listed in Appendix C.*

*Cleaning Jewelry*

*You will need a good buffing machine, sources for which I list in Appendix C. Even if you choose not to buff your jewelry, you should, at the very least, buy a good ultrasonic cleaning machine. You can buy one of these from the same place you buy all your jewelry tools.*

*An ultrasonic jewelry cleaner takes more common sense than skill to operate. Just fill it with water and ammonia (I use a 50/50 mixture), turn it on, and put in your jewelry. I recommend you get one with a heated* tank. The two main things you should remember about ultrasonic machines is that they can shake mounted stones loose if the stones are not tight, and the harsh ammonia can eat up soft stones like opals and pearls. Unless you are trained to repair jewelry, never put a customer's ring in your ultrasonic machine or try to buff it on your buffing machine. Even though I am a trained goldsmith, I have had accidents using both of these machines. My buffing machine once grabbed a large rope chain I was trying to buff and tore the chain to pieces, beating the hell out of my hand in the process. If the chain had belonged to a customer, I would have had to buy him another one.

Before setting your jewelry out for

sale, you should make sure all stones are tight and all the prongs meant to hold them in place are present. If not, get them fixed. Customers get angry when the ring they just bought from you loses a stone the next day. Also make sure all your chains and bracelets have good clasps on them. Basically, all your jewelry should look as close to new as possible.

## Repairing Jewelry

I spent six months at Bowman's Academy to learn basic jewelry repair, but there are now several good two week courses offered in many parts of the country. But the pawnshop business is the perfect place to learn and practice this trade. There will be plenty *of broken and damaged jewelry to practice on, and if you screw up, just scrap your mistakes.*

*I do all jewelry repairs for my pawnshop. When I first opened, I also took in customer jewelry for repair and did ring sizing and mounted stones. This can be an excellent source of extra income for your fledgling business. It also helps to sell your jewelry if people know you are a goldsmith and service the product you sell.*

*If you can't or don't want to repair jewelry or size rings for customers, find a good goldsmith that will do the work for you at shop prices. You can make extra money by charging your customers a few dollars more than your cost.*

*Casting Jewelry*

*A friend of mine who is in the pawn broking business separated the jewelry part from the rest of one of his pawnshops and now offers a full-service jewelry store in conjunction with his pawnshop business. He rarely scraps his old gold. Instead, he melts it and recasts it into new jewelry. This can be a good way to stock your showcase with jewelry, especially when you are just getting started. Even if you aren't inclined to do the work yourself or don't want to buy all the expensive equipment necessary to cast jewelry, you can usually find someone in your area who will do it for you.*

*There are also places that will do this kind of work for you by mail. These are listed in Appendix C. One thing to remember to do when having your scrap cast into jewelry is weigh it before you send it, and weigh it when you get it back. Some reduction in weight is*

These are my showcases with the jewelry trays spread out for sale.

*expected, but it should be less than 5 percent. You will also need to give the goldsmith more gold than it will take to actually make the jewelry so there is enough to completely fill the mold. Just make sure he sends back all the leftovers or gives you credit toward his labor.*

*Displaying Jewelry*

The way you display your jewelry can be very helpful to your sales. I try making my jewelry displays as nice as the jewelry stores'. You will need good glass showcases *that can be locked. Used showcases are the best deal as long as they are clean and presentable. Two 5- or 6-foot long showcases should be plenty to start with. They should have* lights in them. I also use track lights over my showcases with 40-watt spotlights to add sparkle to my diamonds and other gems. They also help highlight the gold jewelry.

It's not necessary to buy all your jewelry displays from expensive wholesalers when you can make most of what you need yourself. Most of my jewelry is displayed on 1-inch-thick 12-by-18-inch Styrofoam boards, which are covered with thick black felt that is stitched or pinned underneath. I have found that black is the best background color to show off gold jewelry.

I use jeweler's U-pins to mount chains and charms for display. The Styrofoam boards are available at your local hobby and craft store, and the U-pins can be purchased from a jewelry supply wholesaler. The black felt is available at any fabric store.

I make my own trays out of Styrofoam and black felt.

I use jeweler's U-pins to mount chains and charms for display. The Styrofoam boards are available at your local hobby and craft store, and the U-pins can be purchased from a jewelry supply wholesaler. The black felt is available at any fabric store.

By cutting the Styrofoam boards to

~ 104 ~

fit smaller spaces in the showcase and on the shelves, I can fill my cases with jewelry. When I'm ready to close at night, these boards can be stacked on top of each other and placed into my safe.

I can also rearrange the chains and charms on the trays to make many different and attractive displays. When I put the boards on the bottom shelf of the showcase, I use felt-covered wood blocks to prop them up in the rear, which gives the customer a better look.

To display rings, I use the same size boards for the base, but I place two 2-by-3-by-12-inch felt-covered blocks on the ends of the boards without attaching them. Then I put rows of model 11v black-on-black ring boxes *(see B. Rush Apple in Appendix C) on the boards between the blocks with their lids open. At the end of the day, I stack the boards so they fit in the safe. Of course, the board on top won't need the blocks, so I can fit a few extra boxes on it.*

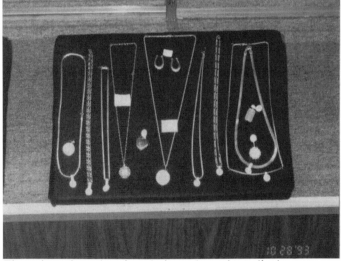

*These boards make nice chain and pendant displays. These pieces are pinned to the board with jeweler's U-pins.*

*I do buy some factory-made ring trays*

~ 106 ~

to display some of my best pieces. These trays usually hold a dozen rings and fit nicely on the uppermost shelves without blocking the view of the jewelry below them. When showing the jewelry in these ring trays, I try to take out only one piece at a time. That way, if the customer is actually a thief and runs with my ring, I will only lose one, not a dozen. I also

*These homemade trays stack nicely to be stored in my safe.*

like to use factory-made trays to

display earrings and small charms. Some charms are hard to tag and have to be put in compartment trays with a price tag on each compartment. It is also best to show these one at a time, because they are so easy to switch around. You must also be careful when handling these trays, because the charms can be knocked into different compartments, causing you to sell a $50 charm for $5.

When you buy price tags, always get sharkskin type tags that can't be torn off easily and have to be cut to be removed. Besides tagging each and every piece of jewelry with a sharkskin price tag, I also put price tags on the lids of my ring boxes so they are clearly visible to my customers. The prices on my chains are also shown clearly. I don't understand why some jewelers and pawnbrokers hide the prices on their merchandise, unless they are ashamed or less than honest. I find that when prices are clearly visible, I save time and trouble. My customers can shop my case and see what is in their price range. When I put my jewelry on sale, the customer can see that I've honestly marked the price down. Also, I am proud of the low prices at which I sell my jewelry.

TIPS ON SELLING JEWELRY

1) Always keep your ring trays full because empty trays encourage thieves. If you show a tray of rings with empty spaces to someone, it is hard to prove how many rings were in the tray.

2) Tag all your jewelry, especially your rings, with price tags, because customers can switch boxes if you let them look at more than one piece of jewelry at a time. (It is a good idea to show only one piece at a time.) You can sell a $500 ring for $50 if it is in the wrong box, even if it is tagged.

3) When showing jewelry to a customer, always look carefully at what they hand back to you, especially if the customer is wearing other pieces of jewelry. It is easy to slip a fake in a ring box undetected. If all your jewelry is tagged with hard-to-remove tags, it is easier to foil these scams.

4) Always keep your showcases locked.

*Some people have long arms with quick hands on the end of them. A whole tray of rings can disappear before you know it.*

*5) Watch out for grab-and-runners. These people will grab and run as soon as you put a tray of expensive rings near their hands.*

*6) Christmas is not only a time for giving, it is also a time for stealing.*

*7) Keep your showcases clean and orderly. People will buy more from a clean display.*

*8) Have a velvet cloth handy to wipe greasy fingerprints off your nice clean jewelry.*

~ 111 ~

9) Buy a small hand-held or countertop mirror so your customers can try on necklaces and see them on their necks.

10) A small magnifying glass will help your customers get a better look at your jewelry.

11) A sales pitch I use to help sell my jewelry is, "If a GIA-certified appraiser doesn't appraise this piece for at least twice what you paid me for it, I'll refund the difference to make it so."

12) If a customer doubts the authenticity of my diamonds or gold, I tell them about my modern electronic testing equipment, and, if necessary, I'll test the item while they watch.

All the above information was printed in 1995 so there are a few revisions, which will be covered in my conclusion.

# Chapter 3

...........................................................

## Conclusion

Buy all diamonds as cheaply as you can. The bottom has fallen out of the market for small diamonds and it is hard to get much for them as scrap. Small single cut diamonds (called "Melee") are virtually worthless as scrap. The last offer I had from a wholesaler for 3 or 4 carats of small diamonds was about 25 cents per point. Unless you need them for repairs it is hardly worth the time and effort necessary to remove them. Larger diamonds have declined in value also. Until you are good at judging the four "C's" then buy as low as you can. Look online for what diamonds and diamond jewelry is selling for. Take a look at Walmart, Sam's Club and any other discount outlets in your area. If want to sell jewelry then you will have to compete with Craig's List, Ebay and the discount stores. If you buy right then you should be able to offer better prices. People are willing to pay a more to established sellers and retail outlets. You need an established clientele that trust you before you will be able get top dollar for your used jewelry. Check out local Jewelers and Pawn Shops in your area. Jewelers that have survived the latest recession and the increase in gold prices should be selling at good prices. Some will be buying gold and silver themselves but many will be interested in items you may want to sell. Find a jeweler who will sell on consignment if you don't have your own store front. He will probably have a goldsmith and a watch maker in house also. Find an honest jeweler and develop a good relationship so you can have your items repaired. Most jewelers will give you dealer prices for repairs if you bring them lots of work just to keep their goldsmiths busy.

I have had great success over the years selling used jewelry to friends, co-workers, neighbors and family. Since you will also be buying from these same folks, the trick is not to offer them the same jewelry you that bought from them. Develop a network of other dealers like yourself that will take your jewelry for consignment and sell it in different markets, that way there is less risk of selling a rerun. This same network can be a source of consignments that you can sell or you can make jewelry trades to vary your inventory.

The gold and silver prices quoted in the original "Pawnbrokers Handbook" have also changed drastically. When the book was written in the mid-nineties, gold was averaging about $350 per ounce. It is now between $1350 and $1400 per ounce. At those prices, there is a fantastic potential for profit. People who bought retail jewelry from me before 2003 can sell it back to me as scrap for more than they paid. I have found that most of the people I buy scrap from are very happy with the prices I am able to offer them. Again, I <u>did not</u> change the price from the original text. Gold prices fall as well as rise and you need to do your own math every time you buy scrap. You will need your calculator.

There are now only two appendixes at the end of this book and any reference to an appendix in my original text will be covered by those.

Remember to trade fairly and honestly with folks. Your good reputation will be an asset to your business. Follow all the laws and pay your taxes.

Finally, I have found that money, possessions, gold and silver did not fill the God shaped hole in my soul. True happiness is not found in wealth. I realized that one day I would die and all the gold and silver that I had acquired would stay above ground and my body would go underground. We work all our lives to dig wealth up, only to leave it and be buried ourselves. There is only one thing that filled me up, Jesus Christ. I have found the Peace that only he can provide. I highly recommend that everyone seek him. By confessing my sins and receiving him into my heart, I now have eternal life. That is something that all the gold and silver in the world or the power they can buy, cannot provide. Jesus Christ, his cross and his blood are the only way to Father God and eternal life with him. I still have gold and silver but I do not put my faith in it, I put my faith in God. I have been investing in his Kingdom and my investment will be waiting for me when I see him. The Bible says a lot about gold, silver, money, investing and how we should use them, pick up a copy and read it. Find a good bible centered Church and give your life to Yeshua Jesus our Messiah. It will be the best investment you will ever make.

God Bless

# Appendix A

Laws Governing Precious Metals Dealers in Virginia

These are the current regulations concerning Precious Metals Dealers in the State of Virginia. Look up the laws that in your state to see what you will need to do the buy scrap gold and silver in your state. There may also be other local laws. I'm sure there are some states and localities that do not require licenses or otherwise regulate buying precious metals scrap but every place will have laws about buying stolen goods. If you buy stolen goods then you are considered to be a "Fence" and the local constabulary will happily prosecute you to the full extent of the law. DO NOT BUY STOLEN GOODS. That being said, most people will stay under the radar if you buy few pieces of jewelry from your friends, neighbors and coworkers. Gold and silver coins are usually exempt from scrap dealers' laws. I'm no Lawyer but I believe the Virginia law also exempts Retail Jewelers and Goldsmiths but I would still comply with law.

§ 54.1-4100. Definitions.
For the purposes of this chapter, unless the context requires a different meaning:
"Coin" means any piece of gold, silver or other metal fashioned into a prescribed shape, weight and degree of fineness, stamped by authority of a government with certain marks and devices, and having a certain fixed value as money.
"Dealer" means any person, firm, partnership, or corporation engaged in the business of (i) purchasing secondhand precious metals or gems; (ii) removing in any manner precious metals or gems from manufactured articles not then owned by the person, firm, partnership, or corporation; or (iii) buying, acquiring, or selling precious metals or gems removed from manufactured articles. "Dealer" includes all

employers and principals on whose behalf a purchase is made, and any employee or agent who makes any purchase for or on behalf of his employer or principal.

The definition of "dealer" shall not include persons engaged in the following:

1. Purchases of precious metals or gems directly from other dealers, manufacturers, or wholesalers for retail or wholesale inventories, provided that the selling dealer has complied with the provisions of this chapter.

2. Purchases of precious metals or gems from a qualified fiduciary who is disposing of the assets of an estate being administered by the fiduciary.

3. Acceptance by a retail merchant of trade-in merchandise previously sold by the retail merchant to the person presenting that merchandise for trade-in.

4. Repairing, restoring or designing jewelry by a retail merchant, if such activities are within his normal course of business.

5. Purchases of precious metals or gems by industrial refiners and manufacturers, insofar as such purchases are made directly from retail merchants, wholesalers, dealers, or by mail originating outside the Commonwealth.

6. Persons regularly engaged in the business of purchasing and processing nonprecious scrap metals which incidentally may contain traces of

precious metals recoverable as a by-product.

"Gems" means any item containing precious or semiprecious stones customarily used in jewelry.

"Precious metals" means any item except coins composed in whole or in part of gold, silver, platinum, or platinum alloys.

(1981, c. 581, § 54-859.15; 1988, c. 765.)

§ 54.1-4101. Records to be kept; copy furnished to local authorities.

A. Every dealer shall keep at his place of business an accurate and legible record of each purchase of precious metals or gems. The record of each purchase shall be retained by the dealer for at least twenty-four months and shall set forth the following:

1. A complete description of all precious metals or gems purchased from each seller. The description shall include all names, initials, serial numbers or other identifying marks or monograms on each item purchased, the true weight or carat of any gem, and the price paid for each item;

2. The date, time and place of receiving the items purchased;

3. The full name, residence address, work place, home and work telephone numbers, date of birth, sex, race, height, weight, hair and eye color, and other identifying marks;

4. Verification of the identification by the

exhibition of a government-issued identification card such as a driver's license or military identification card. The record shall contain the type of identification exhibited, the issuing agency, and the number thereon; and

5. A statement of ownership from the seller.

B. The information required by subdivisions 1 through 3 of subsection A of this section shall appear on each bill of sale for all precious metals and gems purchased by a dealer, and a copy shall be mailed or delivered within twenty-four hours of the time of purchase to the chief law-enforcement officer of the locality in which the purchase was made.

(1981, c. 581, § 54-859.16; 1986, c. 316; 1988, c. 765; 1990, c. 783; 1991, c. 174.)

§ 54.1-4101.1. Officers may examine records or property; warrantless search and seizure authorized.

Every dealer or his employee shall admit to his place of business during regular business hours the chief law-enforcement officer or his designee of the jurisdiction in which the dealer is located or any law-enforcement officer of the state or federal government. The dealer or his employee shall permit the officer to (i) examine all records required by this chapter and any article listed in a record which is believed by the officer to be missing or stolen and (ii) search for and take into possession any article known to

him to be missing, or known or believed by him to have been stolen.
(1991, c. 174.)

§ 54.1-4102. Credentials and statement of ownership required from seller.

No dealer shall purchase precious metals or gems without first (i) ascertaining the identity of the seller by requiring an identification issued by a governmental agency with a photograph of the seller thereon, and at least one other corroborating means of identification, and (ii) obtaining a statement of ownership from the seller.

The governing body of the locality wherein the dealer conducts his business may determine the contents of the statement of ownership.
(1981, c. 581, § 54-859.17; 1986, c. 316; 1988, c. 765.)

§ 54.1-4103. Prohibited purchases.

A. No dealer shall purchase precious metals or gems from any seller who is under the age of eighteen.

B. No dealer shall purchase precious metals or gems from any seller who the dealer believes or has reason to believe is not the owner of such items, unless the seller has written and duly authenticated authorization from the owner permitting and directing such sale.
(1981, c. 581, § 54-859.18; 1988, c. 765.)

§ 54.1-4104. Dealer to retain purchases.

A. The dealer shall retain all precious metals or gems purchased for a minimum of ten calendar days from the date on which a copy of the bill of sale is received by the chief law-enforcement officer of the locality in which the purchase is made. Until the expiration of this period, the dealer shall not sell, alter, or dispose of a purchased item in whole or in part, or remove it from the county, city, or town in which the purchase was made.

B. If a dealer performs the service of removing precious metals or gems, he shall retain the metals or gems removed and the article from which the removal was made for a period of ten calendar days after receiving such article and precious metals or gems.

(1981, c. 581, § 54-859.19; 1988, c. 765.)

§ 54.1-4105. Record of disposition.

Each dealer shall maintain for at least twenty-four months an accurate and legible record of the name and address of the person, firm, or corporation to which he sells any precious metal or gem in its original form after the waiting period required by § 54.1-4104. This record shall also show the name and address of the seller from whom the dealer purchased the item.

(1981, c. 581, § 54-859.20; 1988, c. 765.)

§ 54.1-4106. Bond or letter of credit required of dealers when permit obtained.

A. Every dealer shall secure a permit as required

by § 54.1-4108, and each dealer at the time of obtaining such permit shall enter into a recognizance to the Commonwealth secured by a corporate surety authorized to do business in this Commonwealth, in the penal sum of $10,000, conditioned upon due observance of the terms of this chapter. In lieu of a bond, a dealer may cause to be issued by a bank authorized to do business in the Commonwealth a letter of credit in favor of the Commonwealth for $10,000.

B. If any county, city, or town has an ordinance which regulates the purchase and sale of precious metals and gems pursuant to § 54.1-4111, such bond or letter of credit shall be executed in favor of the local governing body.

C. A single bond upon an employer or principal may be written or a single letter of credit issued to cover all employees and all transactions occurring at a single location.

(1981, c. 581, § 54-859.21; 1988, c. 765.)

§ 54.1-4107. Private action on bond or letter of credit.

Any person aggrieved by the misconduct of any dealer which violated the provisions of this chapter may maintain an action for recovery in any court of proper jurisdiction against the dealer and his surety. Recovery against the surety shall be only for that amount of the judgment which is unsatisfied by the dealer.

(1981, c. 581, § 54-859.22; 1988, c. 765.)
§ 54.1-4108. Permit required; method of obtaining permit; no convictions of certain crimes; approval of weighing devices; renewal; permanent location required.
A. No person shall engage in the activities of a dealer as defined in § 54.1-4100 without first obtaining a permit from the chief law-enforcement officer of each county, city, or town in which he proposes to engage in business.
B. To obtain a permit, the dealer shall file with the proper chief law-enforcement officer an application form which includes the dealer's full name, any aliases, address, age, date of birth, sex, and fingerprints; the name, address, and telephone number of the applicant's employer, if any; and the location of the dealer's place of business. Upon filing this application and the payment of a $200 application fee, the dealer shall be issued a permit by the chief law-enforcement officer or his designee, provided that the applicant has not been convicted of a felony or crime of moral turpitude within seven years prior to the date of application. The permit shall be denied if the applicant has been denied a permit or has had a permit revoked under any ordinance similar in substance to the provisions of this chapter.
C. Before a permit may be issued, the dealer

must have all weighing devices used in his business inspected and approved by local or state weights and measures officials and present written evidence of such approval to the proper chief law-enforcement officer.

D. This permit shall be valid for one year from the date issued and may be renewed in the same manner as such permit was initially obtained with an annual permit fee of $200. No permit shall be transferable.

E. If the business of the dealer is not operated without interruption, with Saturdays, Sundays, and recognized holidays excepted, the dealer shall notify the proper chief law-enforcement officer of all closings and reopenings of such business. The business of a dealer shall be conducted only from the fixed and permanent location specified in his application for a permit. (1981, c. 581, § 54-859.23; 1986, c. 316; 1988, c. 765.)

§ 54.1-4109. Exemptions from chapter.

A. The chief law-enforcement officer of a county, city or town, or his designee, may waive by written notice implementation of any one or more of the provisions of this chapter, except § 54.1-4103, for particular numismatic, gem, or antique exhibitions or craft shows sponsored by nonprofit organizations, provided that the purpose of the exhibitions is nonprofit in nature, notwithstanding the fact that there may be casual purchases and trades made at such exhibitions.

B. Neither the provisions of this chapter nor any local ordinances dealing with the subject matter of this chapter shall apply to the sale or purchase of coins.

C. Neither the provisions of this chapter nor any local ordinance dealing with the subject matter of this chapter shall apply to any bank, branch thereof, trust company or bank holding company, or any wholly owned subsidiary thereof, engaged in buying and selling gold and silver bullion.

(1981, c. 581, §§ 54-859.24, 54-859.27; 1984, c. 583, § 54-859.28; 1988, c. 765.)

§ 54.1-4110. Penalties; first and subsequent offenses.

A. Any person convicted of violating any of the provisions of this chapter shall be guilty of a Class 2 misdemeanor for the first offense. Upon conviction of any subsequent offense he shall be guilty of a Class 1 misdemeanor.

B. Upon the first conviction of a dealer for violation of any provision of this chapter, the chief law-enforcement officer may revoke the dealer's permit for one full year from the date the conviction becomes final. Such revocation shall be mandatory for two full years from the date the conviction becomes final upon a second conviction.

(1981, c. 581, § 54-859.25; 1988, c. 765; 2010, c. 100.)

§ 54.1-4111. Local ordinances.

Nothing in this chapter shall prevent any county, city, or town in this Commonwealth from enacting an ordinance regulating dealers in precious metals and gems which parallels this chapter, or which imposes terms, conditions, and fees that are stricter, more comprehensive, or larger than those imposed by this chapter. In any event, the terms, conditions, and fees imposed by this chapter shall constitute minimum requirements in any local ordinance. Any fee in excess of the one specified in § 54.1-4108 shall be reasonably related to the cost of enforcement of such local ordinance.

(1981, c. 581, § 54-859.26; 1988, c. 765.)

# Appendix B

Sources and Supplies

(All previously mentioned appendices are condensed in this appendix)

Associations

National Pawnbrokers Association
P. O. Box 508
Keller, Texas 76244
Phone: 817-337-8830
Email: info@NationalPawnbrokers.org

Internet: www.nationalpawnbrokers.org
Or http://pawnindustrymarketplace.com
(This is an excellent source for links to gold refiners, silver buyers, jewelry supplies, diamond dealers and other wholesale buyers.)

Books

The following is a list of books that I use and that I highly recommend acquiring.

Beyond the Glitter: Everything You Need to Know to Buy, Sell, Care For, and Wear

Gems and Jewelry Wisely
Gerald L. Wykoff
(This is the best book ever written on this subject. It is well written, easy to understand and is full of need to know knowledge. I believe it may now be out of print but it is still available at Amazon, Ebay or your local Library. )

Or

Beyond the Glitter (Gemology I, Vol. 1)
Gerald L. Wycoff GG CSM Ph.D
(I have not seen this material but I assume it contains the same information that his book does.)
Available online at Amazon and others.

Blue Book of U.S. Coins - Paperback
Whitman Publishing, LLC
3103 Clairmont Road

Suite B
Atlanta, Georgia 30329
800-546-2995
Available online at Amazon and others.

The Official Blackbook Price Guide to United States Coins
Random House, Inc

1745 Broadway
New York, NY 10019
212-782-9000
Available online at Amazon and others

(You can probably get by with either of the above. Most of the coins I see are culls but occasionally a collectable coin with extra numismatic value will show up. )

Coin Dealers Newsletter "Grey Sheet"
CDN
P.O. Box 7939
Torrance, CA 90504
http://greysheet.com
Email: orders@greysheet.com
(This is a wholesale newsletter for Coin Dealers.)

**Diamond Buyers**

Bluestone Trading Company
P.O. Box 24126
Cleveland, Ohio 44124
440-442-7280
888-800-BLUE
Fax: 440-442-0026
        800-321-7979

(I have dealt with Bluestone Trading for many years and I have found them very honest. I do not list other diamond buyers because I have had no dealings with any other but there are several others listed at the NPA Pawn Industry website. )

## Gold and Silver Refiners, Scrap Buyers

Garfield Refining Company
810 East Cayuga Street
Philadelphia, PA 19124
Tel: 800-523-0968
Fax: 215-533-5902
Email: info@garfieldrefining.com
www.garfieldrefining.com

Hoover and Strong
10700 Trade Road
Richmond, Virginia 23236-3000

1-800-759-9997

Fax: 1-800-616-9997

www.hooverandstrong.com

(Hover and Strong has an excellent tutorial
and chart online at;

http://www.hooverandstrong.com/catego
ry/Buying+Jewelry+Scrap )


Kitco Logistics, Inc.

64 Lake Street

Rouses Point, NY 12979

1-888-259-7227

1-518-297-2300

Fax: 1-518-297-2301

www.kitco.com


Midwest Refineries, LLC

4471 Forest Ave.

Waterford, Michigan 48328
1-800-326-2955

Fax: 1-248-674-7305

www.midwestrefineries.com

(I have done business with the above refining companies. There are more listed at the NPA Pawn Industry website. )

**Jewelry Supplies and Tools**

National Jeweler's Supply

101 Mystic Ave

Medford, MA 02155

888-657-8665

www.nationaljewelerssupplies.com

Polishers & Jewelers Supply Corp.

662 Atwells Ave.

P.O. Box 3448

Providence, RI 02909

Tel: 1-401-454-2888

Fax: 1-401-454-2889

www.pjsupply.com

## Silverware Buyers

Atlantic Silver does not seem to be in business any longer and their silver pattern guide went with them.

Beverly Bremer Silver Shop

3164 Peachtree Road N.E.

Atlanta, GA 303005

1-800-270-4009

1-404-261-4009

Made in the USA
Charleston, SC
17 April 2011